AIRBORNE

A Photobiography of Wilbur and Orville Wright

By Mary Collins

NATIONAL GEOGRAPHIC

WASHINGTON, D.C.

STAFF FOR THIS BOOK

Nancy Laties Feresten, *Vice President, Editor-in-Chief, Children's Books*
Bea Jackson, *Art Director, Children's Books*
Jo H. Tunstall, *Project Editor*
Mary Collins, *Illustrations Research*
Marty Ittner, *Designer*
Callie Broaddus, *Associate Designer*
Suzanne Patrick Fonda, *Editor*
Jennifer Emmett, *Editor*
Alex Novak, *Managing Editor*
Paige Towler, *Editorial Assistant*
Lori Epstein, *Senior Photo Editor*
Janet Dustin, *Illustrations Coordinator*
Carl Mehler, *Director of Maps*
Equator Graphics and Gregory Ugiansky, *Map Research and Production*
R. Gary Colbert, *Production Director*
Lewis R. Bassford, *Production Manager*
Vincent P. Ryan, *Manufacturing Manager*
Marla Conn, *Education Consultant*

PUBLISHED BY THE NATIONAL GEOGRAPHIC SOCIETY

Gary E. Knell, *President and CEO*
John M. Fahey, *Chairman of the Board*
Melina Gerosa Bellows, *Chief Education Officer*
Declan Moore, *Chief Media Officer*
Hector Sierra, *Senior Vice President and General Manager, Book Division*

SENIOR MANAGEMENT TEAM, KIDS PUBLISHING AND MEDIA

Nancy Laties Feresten, *Senior Vice President;* Jennifer Emmett, *Vice President,
Editorial Director, Kids Books;* Julie Vosburgh Agnone, *Vice President,
Editorial Operations;* Rachel Buchholz, *Editor and Vice President,* NG Kids
magazine; Michelle Sullivan, *Vice President, Kids Digital;* Eva Absher-Schantz,
Design Director; Jay Sumner, *Photo Director;* Hannah August, *Marketing
Director;* R. Gary Colbert, *Production Director*

DIGITAL

Anne McCormack, *Director;* Laura Goertzel, Sara Zeglin, *Producers;* Emma
Rigney, *Creative Producer;* Bianca Bowman, *Assistant Producer;* Natalie Jones,
Senior Product Manager

National Geographic supports K–12 educators with ELA Common
Core Resources. Visit natgeoed.org/commoncore for more information.

Printed in China
15/RRDS/1

For my parents, who sparked an interest in flight when they
brought their ten-year-old daughter to see the "Red Baron" spin,
loop, and dive at an air show in Rhinebeck, New York.

Special thanks to Jane Wildermuth and the library staff at Wright
State University for their tireless help with the photo research and
to Peter L. Jakab at the National Air and Space Museum for his
expert readings and patience with all our questions.

— M.C.

ILLUSTRATION CREDITS

t–top; c–center; b–bottom; bkgrd–background

NASA–National Air and Space Agency; NASM–National Air and Space
Museum; NMNH–National Museum of Natural History; PLDL–Paul
Laurence Dunbar Library; SI–Smithsonian Institution; WSU–Wright
State University

Front cover and spine, Corbis; back cover, courtesy Library of Congress; 1,
PLDL, WSU; 2-3, courtesy Library of Congress; 5, NMNH, SI; 6, PLDL,
WSU; 9 (t), NASM, SI; 9 (b), NASM, SI; 10 (t), PLDL, WSU; 10 (c), cour-
tesy Library of Congress; 10 (b), PLDL, WSU; 11, PLDL, WSU; 12 (bkgrd),
PLDL, WSU; 12 (inset), PLDL, WSU; 14-15, Underwood & Underwood/
Corbis; 16, courtesy Library of Congress; 17, PLDL, WSU; 18, NASM,
SI; 19 (t) John Ottinger; 19 (b), courtesy Library of Congress; 20, John
Ottinger; 21, PLDL, WSU; 22, PLDL, WSU; 23, PLDL, WSU; 24-25, cour-
tesy Library of Congress; 26 (t), PLDL, WSU; 26 (b), PLDL, WSU; 27 (t),
courtesy NASA; 27 (b), Brown Brothers; 28, PLDL, WSU; 29 (t), courtesy
Henry Ford Museum; 29 (b), NASM, SI; 30-31, PLDL, WSU; 32, PLDL,
WSU; 35, PLDL, WSU; 36-37, PLDL, WSU; 39 (t-bkgrd), NASM, SI; 38
(b-bkgrd), Corbis; 38 (inset), courtesy Library of Congress; 40 (t), PLDL,
WSU; 43 (inset), courtesy Library of Congress; 43 (bkgrd), courtesy Library
of Congress; 45, PLDL, WSU; 46-47, PLDL, WSU; 48, PLDL, WSU; 49,
PLDL, WSU; 50 (bkgrd), PLDL, WSU; 50 (inset), NASM, SI; 52, PLDL,
WSU; 53, PLDL, WSU; 54-55, PLDL, WSU; 56, PLDL, WSU; 57 (t), PLDL,
WSU; 57 (b), PLDL, WSU; 57 (bkgrd), courtesy Franklin Institute; 58,
PLDL, WSU; 61, John Ottinger

COVER: Orville and Dan Tate unleash Wilbur in the 1902
glider at Kill Devil Hills. This particular glider was so
successful it convinced the brothers they could build an
engine-powered airplane.

HALF-TITLE PAGE: Wilbur flies at sunset at Le Mans, France.

TITLE PAGE: The brothers engaged in discussions about every
detail of their flying machine. Here, they converse outside the
hangar at Huffman Prairie with the 1904 Flyer by their side.

PAGE 5: Wilbur and Orville Wright

The National Geographic Society is one of the world's
largest nonprofit scientific and educational organizations.
Founded in 1888 to "increase and diffuse geographic
knowledge," the Society's mission is to inspire people
to care about the planet. It reaches more than 400 million people worldwide each month through its official
journal, *National Geographic,* and other magazines;
National Geographic Channel; television documentaries; music; radio; films;
books; DVDs; maps; exhibitions; live events; school publishing programs;
interactive media; and merchandise. National Geographic has funded more
than 10,000 scientific research, conservation, and exploration projects and
supports an education program promoting geographic literacy.

For more information, please visit nationalgeographic.com, call
1-800-NGS LINE (647-5463), or write to the following address:

NATIONAL GEOGRAPHIC SOCIETY
1145 17th Street N.W.
Washington, D.C. 20036-4688 U.S.A.

Visit us online at nationalgeographic.com/books

For librarians and teachers: ngchildrensbooks.org

More for kids from National Geographic:
kids.nationalgeographic.com

For information about special discounts for bulk purchases, please contact
National Geographic Books Special Sales: ngspecsales@ngs.org

For rights or permissions inquiries, please contact National Geographic
Books Subsidiary Rights: ngbookrights@ngs.org

"…while thousands of the most dissimilar
body structures, such as insects,
fish, reptiles, birds and mammals, were flying
every day at pleasure, it was reasonable
to suppose that man might also fly."

Wilbur Wright

German spectators marvel at Orville flying an invention that would mark the beginning of a new era in transportation.

Foreword

On October 5, 1905, a three-year-old boy named Charley Billman observed a spectacular airplane flight of nearly 40 minutes over a cow pasture near his home in Dayton, Ohio. For weeks afterward, young Charley raced around his parents' house, arms out like wings, copying the sound of an engine. Since then, Charley's playful imitation of an airplane in flight has been repeated by millions of children. Surely all of us have done this at one time or another. Charley, of course, was watching Wilbur and Orville Wright fly their exciting new invention.

Most people have heard of the Wright brothers and know they invented the airplane, but few really know the full story of their impressive accomplishment. With great skill, imagination, and perseverance, they sorted through and solved the many complex problems that human flight presented. They did not simply build one airplane and get off the ground. They built a series of designs, perfected their invention, and in the process became the world's first true aeronautical engineers. Every airplane that successfully flew after the Wright brothers' was based on their ideas and solutions.

The book you hold in your hands tells the amazing story of these two humble men whose hard work helped create the world we live in. The Wright brothers achieved their goal a century ago, but what they did affects our lives every day.

Little Charley Billman was among the first to see an airplane fly. He was also among the first to see the future.

Peter L. Jakab
Curator
National Air and Space Museum
Smithsonian Institution

Wilbur Wright left his bicycle shop carrying the most unusual kite the boys had ever seen. They followed him in the July heat to an open field near the outskirts of Dayton, Ohio, then watched as he pulled the five-foot wings into the sky using cords attached to sticks in his hands. The great mass of wood, cloth, and wires hovered above them, blocking out a patch of the summer sky. Suddenly the kite swooped toward the boys, who dove into the grass to avoid getting hit.

Perhaps Wilbur was having some fun with the children as he swerved his kite up and down in great arcs, but his larger purpose was quite serious. He wanted to prove that changing the angle of the wings would give him more control over the flight of his kite. His tests on that open field in 1899 proved him right. It was one of the thousands of small steps that ultimately enabled him and his younger brother, Orville, to design, build, and pilot the world's first airplane.

Wilbur was born on April 16, 1867, in Millville, Indiana, the third son of Milton and Susan Wright. Three years later Milton Wright, a minister in the United Brethren church, moved his family to Dayton, Ohio, where Orville was born on August 19, 1871. As adults, both had a strong memory of when they first took an interest in flight. "Father brought home to us a small toy actuated by a rubber spring which would lift itself into the air," Orville recalled. He was 7 and Wilbur 11 when their father surprised them with the little helicopter. Neither of them imagined then that one day they would launch themselves into the air in one of the most astounding inventions in the history of the world.

Wilbur, age 13 (top) and Orville, age 9

"… Orville and myself lived together, played together, worked together, and, in fact, thought together . … nearly everything that was done in our lives has been the result of conversations, suggestions, and discussions between us."

WILBUR WRIGHT

Milton Wright was away from home for weeks at a time to work with members of his congregation, who were spread throughout the Midwest. He often brought gifts, such as the little helicopter, home to his five children—Reuchlin, Lorin, Wilbur, Orville, and Katharine—because he missed them so much. To make things easier on himself, he frequently moved the whole family, which meant the Wright children grew up in towns all over the Midwest. All the Wrights were happy in 1884 when they finally settled down for good at 7 Hawthorn Street in Dayton. Sadly, by then, their mother had become very ill with the lung disease tuberculosis.

For years Susan Wright had endured long stretches of time without her husband at home and with five children to care for. She appreciated the value of his church work and did all she could to support it. But the constant moves—12 over 30 years of marriage—were especially difficult because she had to pull the children out of school and leave good friends behind. Descended from a family of German carriage builders, Susan loved working with her hands and often worked on projects with the children. She built them a fine shed when they lived in Iowa and later a homemade sled.

Even though the brothers' mother, Susan (middle), died young, she instilled a love for tinkering in her boys. The father, Milton (top), and sister, Katharine (bottom), did all they could to encourage and support Wilbur and Orville's experiments.

The Wright family lived in many towns in the Midwest before finally settling down in this house at 7 Hawthorn Street in Dayton, Ohio, in 1884.

Toledo

Cleveland

O H I O

★ Columbus

○ **Dayton**

Cincinnati

She encouraged them to be kind and close to each other precisely because they never knew how long they might stay in any one community. School and neighbors might change, she felt, but family ties were forever.

Two years after their final move to Dayton, 18-year-old Wilbur was hit in the face with a stick used to play an ice-skating game called shinny (a little like ice hockey). The accident severely damaged his mouth and caused him tremendous pain for months. Instead of healing quickly and returning to an active life, he withdrew. For four years he stayed close to home to nurse his wounds and to look after his ailing mother. He became so reclusive that his brother Lorin wondered in a letter to Katharine if Wilbur were destined to remain a "cook and chambermaid" all his life.

When his mother died in 1889, Wilbur was 22 and had no idea what to do with his life. His lively younger brother, Orville, then age 17, had started a printing business using a press made from odds and ends from a junkyard and some movable type his father had given him. To make more money, however, he knew he needed to build a bigger, better press. He persuaded Wilbur to help. Together the two built a contraption out

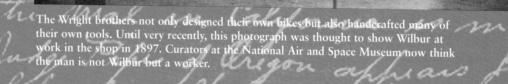

The Wright brothers not only designed their own bikes but also handcrafted many of their own tools. Until very recently, this photograph was thought to show Wilbur at work in the shop in 1897. Curators at the National Air and Space Museum now think the man is not Wilbur but a worker.

of rummaged parts, including the top of an old buggy carriage, that could print 1,000 sheets an hour. In no time they began receiving orders to print small newsletters and other items. When a pressman from Chicago came to visit, he lay on the floor to examine their odd machine. "Well, it works, but I certainly don't see how!" he exclaimed.

Even as they continued to build their printing business, the brothers, especially Wilbur, became restless. By the mid-1880s, bicycles had become a national craze. A new style called the "safety bicycle," with two air-filled tires of the same size (instead of two rigid tires of dramatically unequal size), comfortable seats, and foot brakes made it much easier and safer for people to ride. By 1895, Americans—the Wright brothers among them—had bought 1.2 million bicycles, even though the average worker made only $440 a year and the average adult cycle cost about $50.

Good with their hands and avid riders, the Wright brothers opened a bicycle shop in 1892. In just three years they jumped from selling and repairing bicycles to designing and producing their own custom-made models. Soon the brothers had a solid business that relied on some of the newest technology of the time. Their store in Dayton was as sophisticated for its time as an expensive computer repair and production shop would be today. At the turn of the century a Smithsonian scientist, W. J. McGee, insisted that the bicycle was "one of the world's great inventions." An editorial writer from Boston, James Howard Means, argued that a man involved with bicycles would be the first to invent flight because, "to learn to wheel one must learn to balance. To learn to fly one must learn to balance."

There were lots of bicycle shop owners in the United States in the 1890s. Why did these two young men, Will and Orv (as their family and friends called them), come up with the crucial answers necessary for flight?

The brothers' astounding persistence and focus certainly set them apart. Unlike many of their brilliant counterparts who explored flight, such as Alexander Graham Bell, inventor of the telephone, Wilbur and Orville did not have a host of other scientific projects pressing on their time. They did

"One of the most surprising feats of practical mechanics is that a carriage with but two wheels, propelled by the feet of the rider . . . should maintain an upright position."

Scientific American, SEPTEMBER 23, 1868

By 1892, citizens of Dayton could shop at any of 14 bicycle stores in the city, but if they wanted something custom-made, their best bet was the Wright Cycle Company on W. Third Street.

L. G. KELLER & CO   UNDERTAKERS

not have wives, children, or huge obligations to an institution or large business. Their modest bicycle shop gave them an income and lots of spare time, especially during the fall and winter, when business always trailed off. That meant they could focus all of their intellectual and mechanical skills on one overriding problem: how to fly. They attacked the question creatively and relentlessly until they found answers that made sense.

Orville in particular loved to bang away on his latest idea. Always dressed neatly in a starched collar and tie, he'd don an apron and set to work. Painfully shy among strangers, Orville was a chatty prankster with family and good friends. One day when he was in grammar school, he put a hot pepper in his classroom heater to "spice" up the class. As a grown-up, he wore dapper clothes and sported a reddish mustache. His boyish charm never left him.

Orville Wright

Bald by his late twenties, Will looked more serious and intellectual than his younger brother. Wilbur loved to mull over big ideas, which often left others with the impression that he lived "largely in a world of his own," as one neighbor recalled. Despite his aloof style, Wilbur was more confident dealing with strangers than Orville, so he served as spokesman for both of them.

While Orville would joke around with their nieces and nephews and make candy for them, Wilbur preferred to read to the children.

The younger brother raced bikes and jumped from project to project. The elder brother took comfort in methodical routines and put his hat on the same chair every day when he went home for lunch. Together, the tinkerer and the intellectual made a formidable team—two men with an idea and the mechanical skills to make it real.

The brothers first became serious about building a flying machine in 1896, the year a German engineer named Otto Lilienthal died while testing one of his gliders. Lilienthal had made serious discoveries about wing design and had conducted nearly 2,000 short glides. He was aloft on yet another test flight when he stalled 50 feet in the air, then nose-dived to the ground. He broke his spine and died the next day.

Wilbur Wright

At the time, Orville was recovering from a life-threatening bout of typhoid fever. Will entertained him by reading the newspaper. One day the brothers came across the story announcing the death of the famous "Flying Man." Already interested in flight, the two men discussed the German's work at length. Lilienthal had made real progress with his gliders and often flew for hundreds of feet. What had gone wrong?

Once Orville recovered from his illness, he rejoined Wilbur in the back of the bicycle shop where they began seriously exploring the science of flight. They read books about birds from their local library, but that just left them with more questions. Wilbur wanted answers, so in 1899

Plenty of crackpots had tried to "fly" by the turn of the 19th century, but Otto Lilienthal was one of the few to make intelligent advances in wing design based on careful study. His death after a failed glide in 1896 inspired the Wrights to pursue the answers to flight.

he wrote to the leading national science organization of the time, the Smithsonian Institution in Washington, D.C., and asked for any publications they had on flight.

A Smithsonian staff member sent him several articles and a list of books about flying that included *Progress in Flying Machines*, written by the famous engineer Octave Chanute, who later became their good friend. After reading all that the Smithsonian had sent and several of the recommended books, Wilbur concluded that there was no art of flying but only "a flying problem." Although many men had thought about flying and some had even built what they called flying machines, none of these inventions actually flew. Wilbur concluded that he and Orville would have to come up with most of the answers themselves.

On the day that the boys watched him in the field, Wilbur was testing a revolutionary wing design that would prove critical to the brothers' success. Both men noticed that a rigid wing made it hard to maneuver in the air. Birds clearly flexed their wing tips when they went into a turn, so why not do the same with a glider or airplane wing? But how?

While chatting with a customer at the bicycle shop, Wilbur began absent-mindedly twisting a long cardboard box in his hands. When the shopper left, he glanced down and realized that the twist in the long, thin box might work on a wing. Wilbur constructed a kite to test the technique, which he and Orville eventually called wing warping. By using cord to twist the wings on each side of his kite in opposite directions, Wilbur could generate an unequal amount of lift

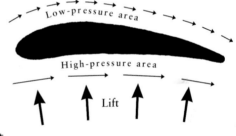

Air tends to bend up and around solid surfaces, which explains why it rushes more quickly over the top of a wing than across the bottom. The difference in acceleration reduces the pressure above the wing and increases the pressure below the wing. The high-pressure area moves into the low-pressure area, which produces lift.

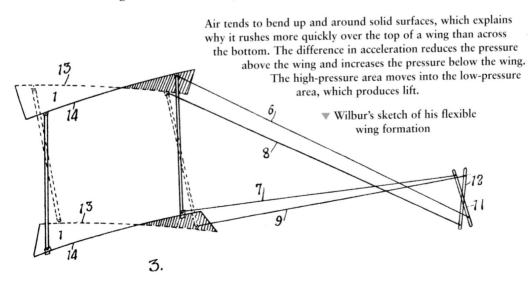

▼ Wilbur's sketch of his flexible wing formation

on either side of the kite. The side with the greater lift would then rise, causing the kite to bank. This flexible design gave Wilbur much greater control over the banking motion—or roll—of the kite.

To control the up-and-down motion of the nose of the kite—or pitch—he added a third small wing called an elevator to the front. When he applied this design to a glider, he could tweak the angle of the elevator which, when combined with wing warping, allowed him to make midair corrections and actually steer the glider.

The other basic movement in flight is called yaw. Yaw is when an airplane spins around its vertical axis. The brothers thought a more flexible rudder would solve the problem, and it eventually did.

In August 1900, Wilbur and Orville built a glider based on their new design ideas. They wanted to test it somewhere with steady winds, a soft place to land, and privacy. Wilbur wrote to the National Weather Service, which sent him information on wind speeds and temperatures at various sites. He and Orville eventually settled on the Outer Banks of North Carolina, the nearly deserted spits of land just off the Atlantic coast, one of the windiest and sandiest places in the United States.

The three major movements of an airplane are pitch, yaw, and roll. Pitch refers to the up-and-down movement of the nose of an airplane. Yaw refers to the side-to-side movement of an airplane as though it were rotating about an imaginary line running from the top of the airplane through the bottom. Roll refers to the movement of an airplane as though it were rotating around an imaginary line running the length of the airplane.

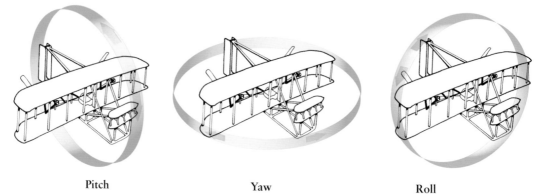

Pitch   Yaw   Roll

Bicycle sales slowed during the fall, so the brothers decided they could take a few weeks off starting in September 1900 to go to North Carolina and try their glider. Wilbur left first, laden with a suitcase, a trunk filled with supplies, a tent, and parts of the glider. Orville was to follow in a week or so. They crated and shipped the rest of the glider.

When Wilbur reached Elizabeth City, North Carolina, it took him three days to find someone willing to ferry him to the Outer Banks, a two-to-three-hour ride on a clear day. The only sailor available owned a boat with rotten sails, "the rope badly worn and the rudder-post half rotted off, and the cabin so dirty and vermin-infested that I kept out of it from first to last," Will wrote Katharine. He climbed aboard anyway because he wanted to get to the tiny fishing village of Kitty Hawk, with its great sandy beaches and dunes.

On the desolate Outer Banks of North Carolina, the Wright brothers found what they needed for their experiments: air, space, soft landings, and solitude.

William Tate, postmaster of Kitty Hawk, North Carolina, poses with his family in 1900. Tate let the brothers stay with him until they set up camp and later volunteered many hours to help haul the Wrights' flying inventions up the dunes.

The wind picked up as a major storm blew in. The boat rolled in the waves, and Wilbur and the sailor had to bail constantly. After hours at sea, they escaped the worst of the storm by sailing into the mouth of the North River, where they spent the night. The next day they made their way to Kitty Hawk. During the two days at sea, Wilbur ate only one thing: a jar of jelly Katharine had snuck into his bag as a surprise.

Wilbur's storm-tossed journey was only the first of the many difficulties the brothers would face. From 1900 to 1902 they returned to the Outer Banks three times to test various gliders. Each time they faced armies of mosquitoes, ticks, snakes, and bedbugs as well as sandstorms, intense heat, cold, and bad weather.

In 1900 they stayed with William Tate, the postmaster, and his family until they could set up camp. They lived in a tent for the rest of that season. In 1901 they built a 17-foot-long shed, which housed both the glider and the two of them. In 1903 they added a second building so they could have a hangar for their glider separate from their living quarters. In their snug little cabin, they slung cots between the rafters and wrapped up in extra blankets on cool nights. Orville played the mandolin for entertainment and Wilbur would join in with his harmonica.

Though their cabin was as tight as they could make it, sometimes the wind blew so fiercely off the ocean that it would tear portions of the roof off. Orville and Wilbur would climb up, nails in hand, and repair it in the rain, then take shelter inside to wait for better weather. They spent far more time waiting than gliding.

Wilbur scours pans with sand outside their tent at Kill Devil Hills, an area of sandy dunes near Kitty Hawk. The brothers shared the camp chores, including cooking, laundry, dishes, and well digging.

Wilbur cooks up a meal in the cramped confines of their 1902 hangar, which housed the inventors and their invention. (The glider can be seen on the right.) In 1903 they built a separate cabin for their living quarters.

"Wilbur and I could hardly wait
for morning to come to get
at something that interested us.
That's happiness!"

ORVILLE WRIGHT

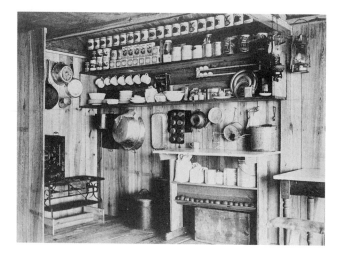

The 1903 cabin had tidy shelves stocked with supplies and cots built into the walls of the loft.

The men from Kitty Hawk who came to watch and often to help, including their friend Dan Tate, the postmaster's half-brother, looked on with concern and disbelief as Will and Orv took off again and again on short hops over the sand. Sometimes the wind would smack the glider's sledlike runners down hard and spray sand into the pilot's nose and eyes. Many who watched thought the brothers were especially crazy because they insisted on lying flat on their stomachs when they flew. Will and Orv knew that lying flat cut down on wind resistance. Some days, when the weather allowed, they took so many test glides their necks ached from holding their heads up.

What were they trying to learn on this windy spit of sand hundreds of miles from home? Right from the start, the brothers figured that an airplane needed three things to fly: a surface like wings to give it lift; an engine to give it power; and a set of controls. Others had worked on wing shapes and engines, but almost no one had explored how to control an airplane once it got into the air. People such as Samuel Langley, Secretary of the Smithsonian Institution, were experimenting with small models of airplanes. Langley spent years working on a machine he called an Aerodrome, which was a scaled-up version of one of his models. It had a much stronger engine than any-

Samuel Langley poses with his pilot, Charles Manly. Below, Langley's Aerodrome takes off from its houseboat launching device and falls into the Potomac River like, as one reporter on the scene commented, "a handful of mortar."

thing the Wright brothers flew, but it plopped into the Potomac River both times a pilot tried to fly it.

The brothers realized early on that air is not a solid road but a very unstable, three-dimensional medium that can be mastered only if a pilot can respond to constant changes. A pilot cannot simply power his way through the turbulence; he must be able to react to it. When the nose of the Lilienthal glider turned down, the only way for Lilienthal to save himself was to have pulled up the front of his craft. He lacked that kind of control so he stalled, dove, and died.

To catch potential problems before they took to the air, the brothers always flew their gliders as kites first. Such methodical testing helped them avoid the fatal accidents that felled many early experimenters. Here, the brothers test their 1901 glider in the sea breezes of the Outer Banks.

From 1900 to 1902, when Wilbur and Orville were not at Kitty Hawk, they were in their bike shop, often arguing about how to perfect the wings and control system of their glider. Charlie Taylor, a mechanic who took charge of their bicycle business when they were away, remembered that "both boys had tempers. They would shout at one another something terrible. I don't think they really got mad, but they sure got awfully hot."

What were they shouting about? Their tests showed that Will's wing-warping idea improved the control of the glider, but nowhere near as much as the brothers had expected, and certainly not enough to make flying a safe undertaking. After the 1901 tests, during which the glider often spun out of control for reasons they didn't understand, they returned to Dayton so disheartened that Wilbur insisted, "Not within a thousand years would man ever fly!"

In August 1901, they resumed their bicycle business. This time, there was no shouting. For weeks there were few exchanges at all in the back of the shop. They worked quietly repairing bikes and catching up on things they had missed while away. Then Wilbur received a letter from Octave Chanute asking if he would give a talk to other engineers about the brothers' work on gliders. Will agreed. While working on that speech, he and Orville began to revisit many of the things that had confused them and decided to do more testing on the shape of their glider's wings.

They made an assortment of wing shapes from tin, wax, and wood, nearly 200 in all. Then they set a bicycle wheel on the handlebars of a bicycle, secured a wing shape to the wheel, and rode as fast as they could up and down the street to see how that specific wing shape reacted in the wind. Once again the bicycle shop owners were giving the local kids something to stare at. Next they made a small wind tunnel out of a starch box and other odds and ends from their shop and tested wing shapes in it. Fascinated by what they were learning, the Wrights made a fancier wind tunnel and wing-testing device out of a six-foot-long wooden box, using bicycle spokes, old hacksaw blades, and a belt-operated fan.

They tested wing shapes for weeks on end. In late August of 1902, they returned to the Outer Banks to test their third glider.

Above is a custom-made Wright bicycle. The odd hub on the handlebars was to help them test wing shapes. The results of these tests convinced them to build a more sophisticated wind tunnel.

Below is a reproduction of their second wind tunnel, built with odds and ends found in their shop and used to test hundreds of wing curvatures.

Two small buildings, lots of
sand, and one man, Wilbur,
contemplating the possibilities
of the 1903 Flyer.

"The newspapers are full of accounts of flying machines which [men] have been building in cellars, garrets, stables and other secret places.... Some of these reports would disgust one, if they were not so irresistibly ludicrous."

WILBUR WRIGHT

Coasting over the sandy expanse of Kill Devil Hills in the 1902 glider, Wilbur Wright makes the world's first controlled turn in a flying machine.

It had a much longer, narrower wing construction based on findings from their wind-tunnel experiments. It also had an improved control system. In the 1900 glider, they had controlled the wing warping with foot pedals while lying flat on their stomachs, an awkward exercise. In 1901, they had developed a clever wooden device they called a hip cradle, which was located where the hips of the pilot would rest and was attached to the wing-warping system. If they swung their hips to the left, the wings on each side of the airplane warped in different directions. The wings on one side tilted up while the wings on the other tilted down. If they moved their hips to the right, the wings warped in the opposite directions. The elevator was controlled with a separate hand lever.

Everything seemed to be going so well until Orville crashed while making a turn. One of the wings had tilted too high and wouldn't come down, which sent the glider into a spin. He walked away unscathed but baffled by the problem.

Orville lay awake one night pondering the glider's tendency to go into a spin. He decided it was because they had no way to alter the angle of the back of the airplane in relation to the wings. The tail should be as movable as the wings, he decided, so it could offset any unexpected side motion.

The next morning he shared his idea with Wilbur, who applauded his great breakthrough. Wilbur then added his own two cents worth: Why not simplify the controls by connecting the hip cradle controls for the wing warping to the movable tail? The brothers now had a way to control their glider up, down, and around—the three dimensions of air.

By the time they left North Carolina in October 1902, they knew they had mastered the most important problems of controlled flight. They still needed to steady the nose of the airplane, plot the shape of the propellers, and build an engine, but the most crucial breakthroughs had been achieved.

At last, they were ready to build and fly a powered airplane.

Over the next few months, Charlie Taylor helped them build a lightweight engine that had about as much horsepower as a small boat engine today. Incorporating the findings from their tests with the 1902 glider, the Wrights built their first Flyer, which Wilbur called the Whopper Flying Machine. Its elegant, spare lines gave it a fragile appearance. It was difficult to control, and the nose had a tendency to turn down.

Will and Orv arrived at the Outer Banks on September 25, 1903, but storm after storm hit the dunes at Kill Devil Hills. They had a terrible time just keeping their cabin from blowing away. In windy isolation they worked on their engine. It had to operate perfectly if they hoped to get their Flyer off the ground. After weeks of testing, they finally felt ready.

"Flight was generally looked upon as an impossibility and scarcely anyone believed in it until he had actually seen it with his own eyes."

ORVILLE WRIGHT

Mankind's first controlled powered flight on December 17, 1903, at Kill Devil Hills, North Carolina, with Orville Wright at the controls

After congratulations all around and a few warm minutes by the fire, they returned to work and made three other flights that historic day. At noon, Wilbur flew 852 feet in 59 seconds, which proved beyond any doubt that they had flown.

Moving the Flyer was exhausting work. While the men were taking a break, a gust of wind flipped the Flyer over and over. Daniels managed to grab it, but the 605 pounds of wire, wood, and cloth just took him along for the ride. By the time the brothers had caught up with their airplane, it was a jumble. After the Wrights had attained worldwide fame, Daniels would joke that he had survived the first airplane crash.

At the time, the damage was no laughing matter to the Wrights. While excited by what they had accomplished, they had hoped to complete even longer flights. With the winter winds blowing and their airplane in need of extensive repair, they knew their first flying season was over. They left for home.

The successful launch of the 1903 Flyer marked a great breakthrough for the Wrights, but they did not consider their work complete. They had solved the basic problems of flight, but they wanted to produce a practical airplane they could sell. That meant they had to build an airplane that could take off from a runway with a passenger or a load of goods.

They decided to end their tests at Kill Devil Hills and begin working near their home in Ohio. In 1904 they convinced a local farmer to allow them to fly at a field called Huffman Prairie. They just had to chase the cows and horses clear of their machine before they tried to take off.

They built another Flyer but found that the field didn't have a steady wind. They'd lay down the wooden rail in one direction, but then the wind would shift and they'd have to start all over again. After months of struggling with just getting off the ground, they decided to build a catapult, which looked like a tower, with 600 to 1,200 pounds of weights attached to a heavy cable. When they released the weights, the cable would propel the Flyer like a stone from a slingshot and, whoosh, they were in the air.

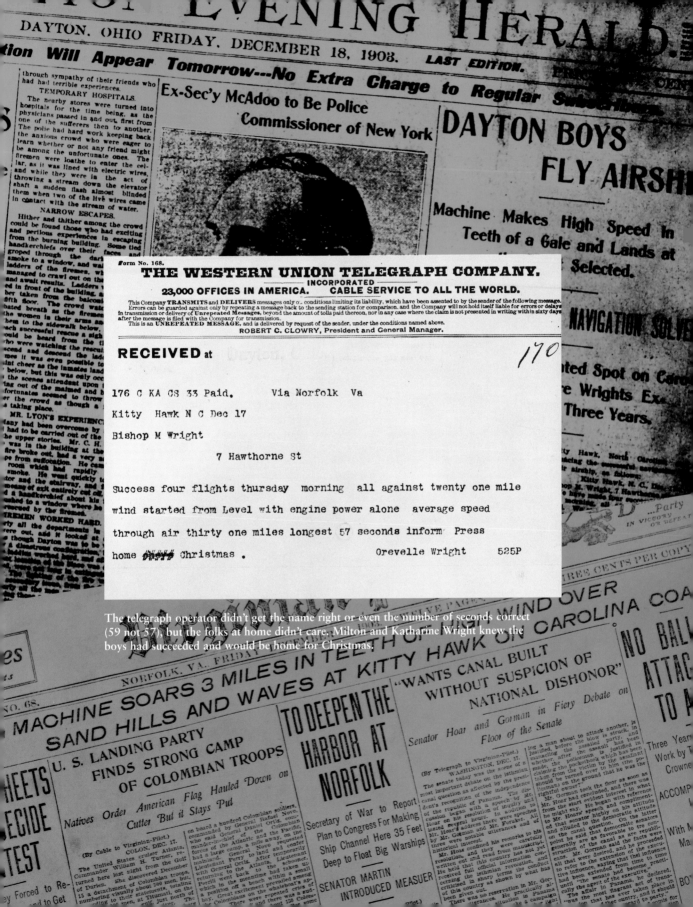

...tion Will Appear Tomorrow---No Extra Charge to Regular Subscribers

Ex-Sec'y McAdoo to Be Police Commissioner of New York

DAYTON BOYS FLY AIRSHIP

Machine Makes High Speed In Teeth of a Gale and Lands at ... Selected.

THE WESTERN UNION TELEGRAPH COMPANY.

INCORPORATED

23,000 OFFICES IN AMERICA.   CABLE SERVICE TO ALL THE WORLD.

This Company TRANSMITS and DELIVERS messages only on conditions limiting its liability, which have been assented to by the sender of the following message.
Errors can be guarded against only by repeating a message back to the sending station for comparison, and the Company will not hold itself liable for errors or delays in transmission or delivery of Unrepeated Messages, beyond the amount of tolls paid thereon, nor in any case where the claim is not presented in writing within sixty days after the message is filed with the Company for transmission.
This is an UNREPEATED MESSAGE, and is delivered by request of the sender, under the conditions named above.
ROBERT C. CLOWRY, President and General Manager.

RECEIVED at Dayton, O.   170

176 C KA CS 33 Paid.   Via Norfolk Va

Kitty Hawk N C Dec 17

Bishop M Wright

7 Hawthorne St

Success four flights thursday morning all against twenty one mile
wind started from Level with engine power alone average speed
through air thirty one miles longest 57 seconds inform Press
home ~~XXXX~~ Christmas .   Orevelle Wright   525P

The telegraph operator didn't get the name right or even the number of seconds correct (59 not 57), but the folks at home didn't care. Milton and Katharine Wright knew the boys had succeeded and would be home for Christmas.

WIND OVER CAROLINA COAST

MACHINE SOARS 3 MILES IN TEETH OF WIND OVER CAROLINA COAST
SAND HILLS AND WAVES AT KITTY HAWK ON CAROLINA COA...

NO. 68.

U.S. LANDING PARTY FINDS STRONG CAMP OF COLOMBIAN TROOPS

Natives Order American Flag Hauled Down on Cutter But it Stays Put

TO DEEPEN THE HARBOR AT NORFOLK

Secretary of War to Report Plan to Congress For Making Ship Channel Here 35 Feet Deep to Float Big Warships

SENATOR MARTIN INTRODUCED MEASURE

"WANTS CANAL BUILT WITHOUT SUSPICION OF NATIONAL DISHONOR"

Senator Hoar and Gorman in Fiery Debate on Floor of the Senate

(By Telegraph to Virginian-Pilot.)
WASHINGTON, DEC. 17.

THREE CENTS PER COPY

NAVIGATION SOLVE...

Frustrated by their inability to get aloft over Huffman Prairie in Ohio, the brothers built a catapult with a cable that ran along a pulley system to the Flyer, which rested on a 60-foot rail. When the pilot unlocked the safety hook in his airplane, the weights would drop and the line would yank the airplane down the rail. Above, a crowd of helpers work to raise the weights of the pulleys on the catapult launching machine.

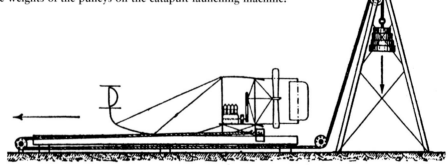

The brothers never worked on Sunday out of respect for their father, now a bishop in the church. But nearly every other day they took a trolley to the field. Most people thought they were crazy to undertake such dangerous work to follow what seemed an impossible dream. One former teacher later recalled seeing them in the trolley cars: "They seemed like well-meaning decent young men. Yet there they were, neglecting their business to waste their time day after day on that ridiculous flying machine."

Will and Orv weren't wasting their time at all but were making major breakthroughs in everything from the complex rotation of the propellers to how to get the most power out of the lightest engine possible. On September 20, 1904, they made their next major breakthrough: Orville flew a full circle around the field. No one had ever sent a heavier-than-air powered machine into the sky and executed a controlled turn.

On that particular day a beekeeper named Amos Root had come out to Huffman Prairie to see what the brothers were up to. People in town had begun to talk about the short glides they were taking. Maybe they really were on to something. On January 1, 1905, Amos reported what he saw in a small newsletter called *Gleanings in Bee Culture*: "I said then, and I believe still, it was…the grandest sight of my life. Imagine a locomotive that has left its track and is climbing up in the air right toward you—a locomotive without any wheels…but with white wings instead.…Well, now, imagine this white locomotive, with wings that spread 20 feet each way, coming right toward you with a tremendous flap of its propellers, and you have something like what I saw."

Even though Orville had succeeded in making a controlled turn, the airplane often had problems with pitch, in which the nose falls in relation to the tail. On July 14, 1905, Orville had a serious accident because of pitch. The Flyer rammed into the ground going 30 miles an hour. Orville walked away with just a few bruises, but the brothers knew it could have been worse. They had to find a solution. Convinced that the answer lay in redesigning the elevator, they worked intensely in the back of their shop testing different designs. They eventually settled on a larger shape placed farther out in front of the wings to make the airplane less tail-heavy. It worked.

Five years after their first serious tests, on October 5, 1905, Wilbur flew their redesigned Flyer 24 miles in 39 minutes over a circular course directly above Huffman Prairie. That was farther and longer than all of their other flights combined. All of their work had come together in a great moment of triumph over a cow field in Ohio.

The world remained largely ignorant of their tremendous advances, and that's how the Wright brothers liked it. They could have staged exhibitions before big crowds on Huffman Prairie, but they didn't. They were afraid that people would steal their ideas. If that happened, they would never be given full credit for their inventions and they could lose the chance to make money from their hard work. Unlike Samuel Langley, who received more than $70,000 in grants from the U.S. government and the Smithsonian Institution to test his experimental airplane, the Wright brothers paid for all their supplies and travel themselves. Tremendously resourceful and frugal, they had built their various gliders and the 1903 Flyer for less than $1,000. The brothers lived at home with their father and sister, made many of the things they needed themselves, and counted their pennies.

To make any profit from their great invention, they needed a government patent for some of the Flyer's most basic features, especially the groundbreaking control system. Only then would others have to pay to use their technology. By November 1905, the brothers believed they had a practical airplane ready to sell. To protect the secrets of their Flyer, they took it apart, stored it, and did not fly again for two and a half years while they sought a patent for "an alleged new and useful improvement in flying machines." The patent finally came through on May 22, 1906.

Wilbur and Orville were already talking with representatives of the U.S. and French governments about selling them airplanes to use for scouting during wartime. Because the brothers were adamant that they would not demonstrate their airplane without a contract, the negotiations were particularly difficult. In 1908, contracts with both governments came through, but they weren't final until the Wrights had demonstrated that their airplanes could meet specific requirements.

For the first time the brothers would have to separate to do their work. Orville would go to Fort Myer in Arlington, Virginia, to fly a sample plane for the U.S. military. Wilbur would go to Le Mans, France, to do the same for the French.

The Wrights recorded data from their experiments in small, shirt-pocket-size notebooks. This 1902 notebook advertised a medicine that would regulate one's liver and was probably a giveaway from a local pharmacy. Orville made the entries on the inside page.

When Wilbur got to Europe in November 1907, he found that he hadn't won everyone's confidence. Newspapers ran headlines like "Liars or Flyers?" and insisted that the Brazilian Santos-Dumont had flown first. Santos-Dumont had built a winged craft he called the *14-bis* that had managed to make a series of short hops in 1906. It didn't come close to what the Wrights had accomplished, but few people in Europe had seen anything better. Wilbur was nothing more than a bluffer, they claimed.

It didn't help that when Wilbur unpacked the crates containing the Flyer he found cracked ribs, torn fabric, and other damage. To make matters worse, the French mechanics on hand to help him had no idea how to work with the unusual motor Charlie Taylor and the Wright brothers had built, which meant Wilbur had to do all the work himself. At one point, while he was tinkering with the engine, a hose broke loose and sprayed him with hot water. Blisters the size of his hand rose on his left arm and side.

With all these troubles, it took Wilbur seven weeks to put the Flyer together. He knew lots of people watching him didn't believe he could fly. Surrounded by doubters, pained by his injuries, lonesome for home, Wilbur pressed on.

On August 8, 1908, as Wilbur told his brother, the day was "the finest for a first trial we have had for several weeks. I thought it would be a good thing to do a little something." That "something" changed the way people saw their world. With the grandstand only partly full, Wilbur had a group of men help him move the completed Flyer out onto the military field at Le Mans, France. They set it on the wooden rail, and he took off, making two successful rounds of the field before landing. Witnesses were stunned. In less than two minutes, Wilbur had shown what it really

Wilbur checked every inch of the 1908 Flyer prior to take off in Le Mans, France. He didn't like to leave even the smallest thing to anyone else.

meant to fly—not lumber through the air and then plop to the ground, but alight into the blue and turn and land gracefully under full control.

Wilbur flew eight more times the following week in front of ever-larger crowds. Men climbed trees to get a better look, then cheered wildly each time he completed a circle in the sky. Newspapers ran huge headlines calling the airplane "The Most Wonderful Flying Machine That Has Ever Been Made." Millions of people learned for the first time ever that humans really could fly. "I've seen him! I've seen them! Yes!" exclaimed one newspaper editor to his readers. "I have today seen Wilbur Wright and his great white bird, the beautiful mechanical bird....There is no doubt! Wilbur and Orville Wright have well and truly flown." The two quiet brothers from Dayton, Ohio, had just become the first international celebrities of the new century.

"The excitement aroused by the short flights
. . . is almost beyond comprehension.
The French have simply become wild.
Instead of doubting that we could do
anything they are ready to believe that
we can do everything."

WILBUR WRIGHT

French farmers pause by their oxcarts in 1909
for the view of a lifetime: Wilbur Wright sailing
overhead in his great, white flying machine.

This cartoon advertisement captures Wilbur's modest but gentlemanly style, including the hat, which the French dubbed a "Veelbur" cap. His successful flights set off a fashion craze as hundreds of thousands of French bought Veelbur caps of their own.

News of Wilbur's accomplishments made its way back to the United States, where Orville was having an easier start than his older brother had had in France. Orville put the Flyer together at Fort Myer in just a few weeks. Because his first short flight took place after Wilbur's great success in Europe, there wasn't as much fanfare. But with each passing day Orville pushed the airplane harder until he flew for 57.5 minutes, a new world endurance record. Now all the headlines were about his exploits.

To fulfill his contract with the U.S. military, Orville had to show that he could carry a passenger, so he began some practice runs. On September 17, 1908, Lt. Thomas Selfridge was in the passenger seat when Orville noticed a strange popping noise that he'd never heard before. (Investigators later learned the propeller had cracked). Selfridge turned pale as he watched Orville working desperately to get the controls to respond. The Flyer dove toward the ground with tremendous speed, then crumbled on impact. The crowd rushed toward the wreckage. Soldiers worked frantically to clear a path for emergency personnel, who carried Selfridge and Orville out on stretchers. Orville's head, back, and hip were injured. Selfridge died a few hours later after surgery failed to save him. When Katharine heard of the accident, she quit her teaching job at a Dayton high school and went to Arlington to nurse her brother, who remained in the hospital for seven weeks.

By himself in France when he heard the news of Orville's brush with death, Wilbur cancelled all his flights for the day and went off alone. He thought about going home, but once he knew his brother would recover, he decided he could accomplish more if he stayed in France and flew for both of them. Wilbur began taking on passengers as well to prove that it could be done. One of those brave volunteers, Maj. Baden Fletcher Smyth Baden-Powell, left a written account of the experience: "Then the driver bends down and releases the catch which holds the anchoring wire. The machine is off!...Mr. Wright, with both hands grasping levers, watches every move, but his movements are so slight as to be almost imperceptible.... All the time the engine is buzzing so loudly and the propellers humming so that after a trip one is almost deaf."

Wilbur returned to the States in 1909 and helped Orville prepare

The brothers knew they risked injury, even death, every time they took a trial flight in their experimental airplane. When a propeller broke during a test run at Fort Myer, the Flyer crashed, severely injuring Orville and killing his passenger, Lt. Thomas Selfridge. Here, men are lifting a portion of one wing.

Jet set in more ways than one! The world's first female airplane passenger, Madame Hart O. Berg, inspired a new skirt style in France when she protected herself against possible "moral hazards" by tying her dress closed prior to takeoff in 1908.

In the background, crowds of children and adults line up to see Orville fly at Tempelhof Field in Berlin, Germany, in 1909.

to restage his test flight at Fort Myer. By July 30, the younger Wright was back at the airplane controls on the takeoff field in Virginia with a lightweight soldier named Benny Foulois as his official passenger. "The air was bumpy," Foulois recalled. "I had the feeling that there were moments when Orville didn't have full control of the machine as we dipped groundward." At times they brushed the treetops, but Orville stayed aloft for the required ten-mile loop and landed safely back at Fort Myer.

The next year, for the first and only time, the two brothers flew together. They had promised their father they would never risk both of their lives in the air at once, but by May 25, 1910, their most important work was behind them. They had taught the world how to fly. As their dad looked on, they sailed over Huffman Prairie with Orville at the controls.

They stayed aloft for six minutes and must have felt such a sense of accomplishment with the wind rushing past their faces and the sound of the motor thrumming in their ears. Later the same day, Orville took their 81-year-old father on his first flight. As they circled the field, Milton Wright urged his son on, "Higher, Orville, higher!"

By this time the two brothers had founded the Wright Company, which manufactured airplanes and trained pilots to perform in air show exhibitions. Neither of them wanted to run the day-to-day operations of a million-dollar company or to deal with the endless lawsuits involving the patent on their Flyer, but these tasks took over their lives nevertheless. Wilbur, in particular, spent a good deal of time in courtrooms in Europe, New York, and Boston to ensure that other aeronautical manufacturers would have to pay to use the technology they had developed.

"We wished to be free from business cares so that we could give all our own time to advancing the science and art of aviation, but we have been

Orville has the ear of his elder brother as they stroll at an air show in New York in 1910.

compelled to spend our time on business matters instead during the past five years," Will complained to a friend in 1911. The following year, already exhausted by so much traveling and wrangling, Wilbur fell ill with typhoid fever and died on May 30, 1912.

In his diary, Milton Wright wrote of his beloved son, "This morning at 3:15, Wilbur passed away, aged 45 years, 1 month, and 14 days. A short life, full of consequences. An unfailing intellect, imperturbable temper, great self-reliance and as great modesty, seeing the right clearly, pursuing it steadfastly, he lived and died."

By the afternoon of May 30, the Wright family had already received more than 1,000 telegrams of sympathy and enough flowers to fill a modern moving van. They wanted a private funeral for Wilbur, such a private man himself, but his international fame made that impossible. Twenty-five thousand people arrived on the clear spring day when he was buried.

Orville had to step up as president of the Wright Company, but he liked the bureaucratic work of a business even less than his older brother had. He purposely set up his office at the bike shop rather than at the company's headquarters. His ferocious secretary, Mabel Beck, kept unwanted visitors at bay.

For the next two years Orville worked on developing an automatic stabilizer that would balance the airplane without any input from the

On June 10, 1909, the Wright brothers and their sister, Katharine, went to the White House, where President William Howard Taft (center) presented them with a gold medal from the Aero Club of America.

pilot. In 1914 he showcased his latest invention by flying seven circles over Huffman Prairie with no hands on the controls in front of members of the famous aviation group, the Aero Club of America. But even this breakthrough was short-lived. Just one year later, Glenn Curtiss's company, the Wright brothers' primary competition, produced a better system. It became the prototype for the industry. By 1915 the Curtiss Aeroplane Company, not the Wright Company, was the largest aircraft manufacturer in the United States.

In 1915, at the age of 44, Orville quit as president and sold his share in the company. In a one-story laboratory he built for himself around the corner from the old bike shop, he tinkered with whatever took his fancy. One year it might be an airplane that could take off and land on water, but another year it might be something as playful as a wooden toy he made for his nieces and nephews that he called "Flips and Flops."

"The whistles of the passing tugs and ferry boats were tooting a mighty chorus and the Battery sea wall was black with people.... from the windows of the towering buildings thousands forgot all else and watched the huge artificial bird sailing up the river."

New York Times, OCTOBER 5, 1909

In an airplane that looks like a fragile dragonfly against the concrete and steel silhouette of New York City, Wilbur Wright performs before more than a million spectators in 1909.

Orville's pet Saint Bernard, Scipio, hitches a ride in the family canoe on Lake Huron in Canada.

In the toy, a trigger released a spring that sent a clown flying off a seat up into the air toward a trapeze, which the little wooden man caught with his wire-hook arms. His brother Lorin sold "Flips and Flops" nationwide. To other aviators of the day, toy making seemed like odd work for one of the founding fathers of flight.

Always shy in front of strangers, Orville continued to withdraw. In 1916 he rented a house for the summer on Waubeck Island, which overlooked Georgian Bay in Canada. He liked the area so much that he bought a nearby island, Lambert Island, before he returned to Dayton in the fall. Katharine, Orville, and their nieces and nephews spent a lot of time in his northern retreat during the warmer months.

In February 1917, he bought a Saint Bernard puppy that he called Scipio. When Milton Wright died a few weeks later on April 3 at age 88, Orville drew even closer to his inner family circle and his pet. Scipio eventually grew to weigh 150 pounds and spent many hours lounging with his owner on the porch at their home in Dayton and on the Wright property in Canada.

The one thing that kept Orville in the news was the Smithsonian's insistence that the ungainly Aerodrome, built by Samuel Langley, had been capable of flight. Egged on by Glenn Curtiss, who altered the wing formation, engine, and other key parts of the original airplane and then flew it as proof that it could fly, the Smithsonian declared the Aerodrome

A man works on a wing frame while a woman stitches a cloth wing cover at the Wright brothers' airplane manufacturing company in Dayton, which the brothers founded in 1909. By 1915, Wilbur had died, Orville had sold his interests in the company, and many competitors had entered the market.

The background is a sketch of the 1903 Flyer drawn by Wilbur on brown wrapping paper. The edge of a wing peeks out at the left edge of the photograph of the woman sewing.

Orville and Katharine share a quiet moment on the porch of Hawthorn Hill, the large house they built in Dayton after the brothers' success. Orville was extremely close to his sister and was brokenhearted when she left both home and Dayton to marry in 1926.

the first airplane and hung it at the Institution. Outraged, and after years of protest, Orville sent the Wrights' 1903 Flyer to the Science Museum in London. Americans were horrified that such a vital piece of their country's heritage was now overseas.

For 30 years the two sides fought. Orville refused to give the Smithsonian the Wright Flyer unless the Institution admitted it had lied about the Aerodrome's successes and bestowed proper recognition on the Wrights. In 1942, the Smithsonian published a paper that acknowledged the changes that had been made to the Aerodrome and recognized the Wright brothers as the first to fly. Orville sent for the Flyer, but agreed to have it shipped after the war when shipping was safer.

On January 27, 1948, Orville suffered a heart attack while at his lab in downtown Dayton. Three days later he died. He was 76 years old. Schools closed. City workers went home. Flags flew at half-staff. On the day of his funeral, four fighter jets flew over his gravesite.

The Science Museum finally shipped the Flyer from England to the Smithsonian Institution. To make way for their new acquisition, the Smithsonian had to move *The Spirit of St. Louis,* the airplane in which Charles Lindbergh made the first crossing of the Atlantic Ocean, from the center of the main hallway of the Smithsonian National Museum to the side.

On December 17, 1948, exactly 45 years after the Wright Flyer took off from the sands near Kitty Hawk, the Smithsonian Institution held a great celebration. As a visiting crowd looked on, the 1903 Flyer was hoisted into position. By day's end, the world's first airplane hovered in the heart of the nation's leading scientific institution, a tribute to the tremendous creativity and perseverance of two brothers from Ohio.

Afterword

Orville Wright flew for the last time as a pilot in 1918. He went up in a 1911 Wright Flyer while another pilot pulled alongside him in a sleek European-style de Havilland DH-4 bomber produced in the same Wright factory. The newsmen on the ground were awestruck by this dramatic example of the rapid changes in aircraft design. But all the snazzy alterations in style masked one basic fact: the Wright brothers' fundamental advances remained the foundation of the de Havilland DH-4, just as they do for all airplanes today.

On the 1903 Wright Flyer, everything looks backwards to us. The huge elevator looms awkwardly out front while the propellers whirl in the back. And what about the landing gear? The earliest Flyer rested on a small truck that ran along a rail for takeoff and landed on sledlike runners. Once, Wilbur even attached a canoe underneath just in case he had to land on the Hudson River while circling New York City.

Today, airplanes set down on tires, a switch the Wright brothers later made in their own models. The tail assembly, called the empennage, contains the elevator, vertical and horizontal stabilizers, and the rudder. The elevator and rudder play the same roles they played in the Flyer, though they are no longer so obvious.

Today, ailerons perform the same function as wing warping and control an airplane's roll. An aileron is a portion of an airplane wing that can be raised or lowered and is located on the trailing edge of the wing. A pilot can move a stick or turn a wheel in the cockpit to make the ailerons move up or down, depending on how he or she wants the airplane to turn. If, for example, a pilot wants to make an airplane turn

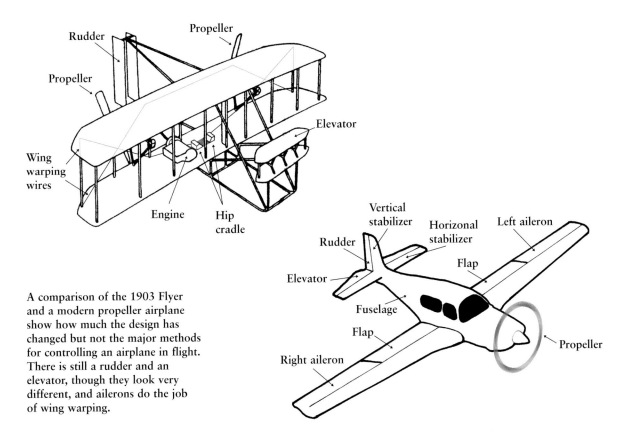

A comparison of the 1903 Flyer and a modern propeller airplane show how much the design has changed but not the major methods for controlling an airplane in flight. There is still a rudder and an elevator, though they look very different, and ailerons do the job of wing warping.

right, he or she will drop the left aileron and raise the right aileron, which will create more lift on the left side of the plane. When coordinated with the rudder, the left wing will move up while the right wing moves down, and the airplane will turn to the right.

The Wright brothers were the first to realize that to solve the mystery of flight they had to break the problem down piece by piece. What sort of curvature should the wings have? Which direction should the propellers spin? How light may a motor be and still provide enough power? They methodically attacked each problem until they had an answer, then moved to the next one. Inch by inch they put together their Flyer. While their vision was grand, their work was painstakingly routine. They tinkered and sweated over every bolt, every stitch. It is precisely because they were so grounded in their scientific method that they were able to discover the secrets of flight and teach the world to fly.

Chronology

April 16, 1867

Wilbur Wright is born in Millville, Indiana.

August 19, 1871

Orville Wright is born in Dayton, Ohio.

1884

After moves to many towns throughout the Midwest, the Wrights settle in Dayton, Ohio, and stay there.

1889

Orville quits school and starts a printing business. Wilbur soon joins him.

1892

Wilbur and Orville open a bicycle shop in downtown Dayton

1896

After the death of the famous glider pilot, Otto Lilienthal, Orville and Wilbur become interested in conducting their own flying experiments.

1899

Wilbur builds and tests a kite that incorporates some important changes in wing design that permit more control of the flight of the kite.

September 1900

The brothers build their first glider, which incorporates the new wing controls and other innovations, and test it at Kill Devil Hills near the small town of Kitty Hawk, North Carolina.

July & August 1901

Wilbur and Orville return to Kitty Hawk to test their new 1901 glider, which does not perform well. On their return to Dayton, they begin to conduct extensive tests on wing designs.

August–October 1902

The brothers test their third glider at Kill Devil Hills and find that their newly designed wings, rudder, and other changes provide much better lift and control. They determine that they're ready to build a motorized airplane, which they call their Flyer.

December 17, 1903

Orville makes the first successful powered airplane flight at Kill Devil Hills, covering 120 feet in 12 seconds. On the fourth and best flight of the day, Wilbur flies for 59 seconds and covers 852 feet.

1904

Wilbur and Orville decide to work on the Flyer near their home in Dayton in a farmer's field called Huffman Prairie.

October 5, 1905

Wilbur flies 24 miles in 39 minutes, marking their greatest achievement to date in the air. They now have a practical airplane that can be sold.

May 22, 1906

Wilbur and Orville receive a patent on the control mechanisms in their airplane.

1908

The Wright brothers finally secure contracts to build planes for the United States military and the French government. Wilbur sails to Europe to conduct demonstration flights for the French. Orville takes charge of the tests for the U.S. military at Fort Myer, Virginia. As the world finds out about their invention, they become international celebrities.

1909

The brothers set up the Wright Company for the manufacture and sale of their Flyers.

May 30, 1912

Wilbur dies of typhoid fever at age 45. Orville takes over the company.

1915

Orville steps down as director of the company to conduct his own research in a small laboratory near the old bicycle shop.

March 3, 1932

A national monument to the Wright brothers is dedicated at Kill Devil Hills, just outside Kitty Hawk, North Carolina. Orville attends the ceremonies.

January 30, 1948

Orville dies at age 76.

Resources

BOOKS

*An * indicates a book of special interest to young adults.*

Anderson, David, and Scott Eberhardt. *Understanding Flight.* McGraw-Hill, 2001.

Combs, Harry, with Martin Caidin. *Kill Devil Hill: Discovering the Secret of the Wright Brothers.* Houghton Mifflin, 1979.

*Corn, Joseph. *The Winged Gospel: America's Romance With Aviation 1900-1950.* Oxford University Press, 1983.

Crouch, Tom. *The Bishop's Boys: A Life of Wilbur and Orville Wright.* W.W. Norton, 1989.

Culick, Fred E. C., and Spencer Dunmore. *On Great White Wings.* Hyperion, 2001.

*Freedman, Russell. *The Wright Brothers: How They Invented the Airplane.* Holiday House, 1991.

Geibert, Ronald, and Patrick Nolan. *Kitty Hawk and Beyond: The Wright Brothers and the Early Years of Aviation.* Wright State University Press, 1990.

Gimbel, Richard. *The Genesis of Flight: The Aeronautical History Collection of Col. Richard Gimbel.* University of Washington Press, 2000.

Hallion, Richard. *The Wright Brothers: Heirs of Prometheus.* National Air and Space Museum, 1978.

*Harris, Sherwood. *The First to Fly: Aviation's Pioneer Days.* Simon and Schuster, 1970.

Howard, Fred. *Wilbur and Orville Wright: A Biography of the Wright Brothers.* Dover Publishers, 1987.

Jakab, Peter L. *Visions of a Flying Machine: The Wright Brothers and the Process of Invention.* Smithsonian Institution Press, 1990.

Jennings, Terry. *Planes, Gliders, Helicopters and Other Flying Machines.* Larousse Kingfisher Books, 1995.

*Kelly, Fred C., ed. *Miracle at Kitty Hawk: The Letters of Wilbur and Orville Wright.* Da Capo Press, 1996.

*Lopez, Donald. *Flight.* Time-Life Books, 1995.

Moolman, Valerie. *The Road to Kitty Hawk.* Time-Life Books, 1980.

Reynolds, Quentin. *The Wright Brothers: Pioneers of American Aviation.* Random House, 1950.

Scott, Phil. *The Pioneers of Flight: A Documentary History.* Princeton University Press, 1999.

*Sobol, David. *The Wright Brothers at Kitty Hawk.* Scholastic Books, 1961.

Taylor, Michael. *Great Moments in Aviation.* Mallard Press, 1989.

Wragg, David. *Flight Before Flying.* Osprey, 1974.

Wright, Orville. *How We Invented the Airplane.* David McKay, 1953.

WEB SITES

Franklin Institute
www.fi.edu

Henry Ford Museum and Greenfield Village
www.hfmgv.org

Library of Congress
www.loc.gov

The National Air and Space Museum
www.nasm.si.ed

The Wright Brothers Aeroplane Company
www.first-to-fly.com

Wright State University
www.wright.edu

INTERVIEWS

Godfrey, Mark, pilot. Telephone conversation with author, May 2002.

Snelgrove, Donnie, former Air Force fighter pilot. Conversation with author, August 2001.

VIDEO

Biography: Wilbur & Orville Wright: Dreams of Flying. A&E Television Networks, 1994.

SOURCES FOR QUOTATIONS

Page 5: Crouch, 161; Page 8: Crouch, 57; Page 9: Crouch, 49-50; Page 11: Howard, 7; Page 13: Crouch, 96, 106, and 115; Page 14: *Scientific American*, Sept. 23, 1868; Page 16: Freedman, 5; Page 19: Culick & Dunmore, 26; Page 21: Howard, 42; Page 25: Crouch, 228; Page 27: Culick & Dunmore, 71; Page 28: Crouch, 243 and Howard, 67; Page 31: Kelly, 61; Page 34: Crouch, 267; Page 36: Crouch, 429; Page 40: Crouch, 282; Page 41: Scott, 136; Page 42: U.S. patent issued to Wilbur and Orville on May 22, 1906; Page 44: Crouch, 366; Page 45: Crouch, 368; Page 46: Kelly, 296; Page 49: Crouch, 381-82; Page 51: Crouch, 398, 12, and Kelly, 447; Page 52: Combs, 345; Page 54: "Wright Flies Twenty Miles," *New York Times*, October 5, 1909, p. A1.

Index

Educational Extensions

1. What characteristics do you think make Wilbur and Orville two of the most interesting and influential men of the 20th century? Why were they considered "eccentric"? Use textual evidence to support your answers.

2. Use evidence from the text to explain what the author meant by "This book you hold in your hand tells an amazing story of these two humble men who helped create the world we live in. The Wright brothers achieved their goal a century ago, but what they did affects our lives every day." Include specific ideas, solutions, and accomplishments that have impacted human flight.

3. How do success and failure relate to each other? Use evidence from the text to show relationships between the two concepts. Discuss specific failures that led to success for the Wright brothers.

4. How did the Wright brothers discover the secrets of flight and share their knowledge with the world? Compare and contrast a modern propeller airplane to the 1903 Flyer.

More to ponder …

- What scientific and historic concepts or ideas are presented in the book? How does the author use evidence to support claims?

- What concepts or ideas would you like to learn more about?

- Who are the inventors that shaped and continue to shape our society?

- How do inventions affect our daily lives?

- What do inventors from the past and present have in common?